IT'S TIME TO EAT HORNED MELONS

It's Time to Eat HORNED MELONS

Walter the Educator

Silent King Books
A WhichHead Entertainment Imprint

Copyright © 2024 by Walter the Educator

All rights reserved. No part of this book may be reproduced in any manner whatsoever without written per- mission except in the case of brief quotations embodied in critical articles and reviews.

First Printing, 2024

Disclaimer

This book is a literary work; the story is not about specific persons, locations, situations, and/or circumstances unless mentioned in a historical context. Any resemblance to real persons, locations, situations, and/or circumstances is coincidental. This book is for entertainment and informational purposes only. The author and publisher offer this information without warranties expressed or implied. No matter the grounds, neither the author nor the publisher will be accountable for any losses, injuries, or other damages caused by the reader's use of this book. The use of this book acknowledges an understanding and acceptance of this disclaimer.

It's Time to Eat HORNED MELONS is a collectible early learning book by Walter the Educator suitable for all ages belonging to Walter the Educator's Time to Eat Book Series. Collect more books at WaltertheEducator.com

USE THE EXTRA SPACE TO TAKE NOTES AND DOCUMENT YOUR MEMORIES

HORNED MELONS

It's time to eat, let's take a look,

It's Time to Eat
Horned Melons

A fruit so spiky, like from a book!

Horned melons, bright and orange to see,

A treasure of nature, just for me.

Their skin is bumpy, their spikes are neat,

A funny fruit that's so unique!

Inside they're green, with seeds that glow,

A jelly-like treat that's fun to show.

Grab a spoon and scoop it out,

What's inside will make you shout!

Tangy, sweet, and a little slimy,

A flavor that's just so yummy and zesty!

They're perfect snacks on summer days,

Cooling bites in sunshine rays.

A fruit that's fun to hold and share,

Horned melons are beyond compare!

It's Time to Eat
Horned Melons

They come from fields where warm winds blow,

A gift of the earth that loves to grow.

From far-off lands, they've traveled here,

To bring us joy and bring us cheer.

Mix them in with other fruit,

A rainbow salad, fresh and cute!

Or just eat plain, right off the spoon,

Horned melons make a perfect tune.

Their seeds are fun to crunch and chew,

A snack for me, a snack for you!

Healthy, bright, and full of fun,

A treat that's good for everyone.

So don't be shy, give it a try,

This spiky fruit is worth your time.

Its look might seem a bit bizarre,

It's Time to Eat
Horned Melons

But inside, it's a tasty star!

The horned melon says, "Come and see,

A world of flavor waits with me."

So gather 'round and take a bite,

It's horned melon time tonight!

When you're done, don't throw away,

The seeds can grow another day.

Plant them deep and watch them sprout,

It's Time to Eat
Horned Melons

Horned melons will come back, no doubt!

ABOUT THE CREATOR

Walter the Educator is one of the pseudonyms for Walter Anderson. Formally educated in Chemistry, Business, and Education, he is an educator, an author, a diverse entrepreneur, and he is the son of a disabled war veteran. "Walter the Educator" shares his time between educating and creating. He holds interests and owns several creative projects that entertain, enlighten, enhance, and educate, hoping to inspire and motivate you. Follow, find new works, and stay up to date with Walter the Educator™

at WaltertheEducator.com

www.ingramcontent.com/pod-product-compliance
Lightning Source LLC
LaVergne TN
LVHW052012060526
838201LV00059B/3998